ALSO BY CALVIN TRILLIN

a HECKUVA job

CALVIN TRILLIN

a HECKUVA job

MORE OF THE
Bush Administration
IN RHYME

RANDOM HOUSE / NEW YORK

Copyright © 2006 by Calvin Trillin

Published in the United States by Random House,
an imprint of The Random House Publishing Group,
a division of Random House, Inc., New York.

RANDOM HOUSE and colophon are
registered trademarks of Random House, Inc.

Most of the poems in this work were previously published in *The Nation*.
Part 2 appeared previously in *The New York Times*.
Some poems in Part 3 were previously broadcast on National Public Radio.

LIBRARY OF CONGRESS CATALOGING-IN-PUBLICATION DATA

Trillin, Calvin.
  A Heckuva job: more of the Bush administration in rhyme / Calvin Trillin.
    p.   cm.
  ISBN 1-4000-6556-9
  1. Bush, George W. (George Walker), 1946– —Poetry.
2. United States—Politics and government—2001– —Poetry.
3. Republican Party (U.S.: 1854–)—Poetry.
4. Presidents—United States—Poetry.   5. Political poetry, American.   I. Title.
PS3570.R5H43 2006
811'.54—dc22   2006043883

Printed in the United States of America on acid-free paper

www.atrandom.com

987654321

FIRST EDITION

Book design by Casey Hampton

CONTENTS

a HECKUVA job

"Brownie, you're doing a heckuva job!" From the moment President George W. Bush uttered that phrase—to Michael Brown, the director of the Federal Emergency Management Agency—we knew that it would be attached to his presidency forever, in the way "The only thing we have to fear is fear itself" is attached to the presidency of Franklin D. Roosevelt. It was instantly recognizable as quintessential George W. Bush: the nickname, the Deke-house bonhomie, the blithe disregard for the obvious fact that Michael Brown, perhaps the only federal official more dilatory than the President himself in rising to the challenge of Hurricane Katrina, had demonstrated stunning ineptitude in a job for which he had no qualifications. What tied it all together was "heckuva," that preppy-on-the-range locution that conjures up just-folks but doesn't offend the sensibilities of fundamentalist Christians. The "heckuva" brought back to me warm memories of the President's father: during a 1988 campaign visit to a drug rehabilitation center, the elder Bush said to one of the residents, "Did you come here and say, 'The heck with it. I don't need this darn thing'?" That, to George H. W. Bush, was depraved doper talk.

Yes, I said warm memories of the President's father. I've often said that each presidential administration makes me nostalgic for the administration that preceded it. In this case, though, the family connection extended the nostalgia to two administrations back. These days, I sometimes wonder how I could have made ungenerous comments about that George H. W. Bush White House team I used to think of as a clutch of Protestant gentlemen in suits. I wonder how I could have failed to recognize, say, the intermittently dozing Brent Scowcroft as a man I'd someday embrace as an ally. I wonder how I could ever have uttered an unkind word about President George H. W. Bush—a former Planned Parenthood enthusiast who was always suspected by the Christian Right of not being a true believer, a commander in chief whose idea of a country we could invade without first putting together a serious international alliance was Panama, a statesman who wrote (with my man Scowcroft) that continuing on to Baghdad to remove Saddam Hussein in 1991 would have made us "an occupying power in a bitterly hostile land," a president who was, blessedly, unafflicted with what he called "the vision thing." We now know that having a cockamamie vision thing is not preferable to having no vision thing at all. In nostalgic moods, I find myself clinging to some lines of a poem I wrote when I was feeling most sympathetic to the first President Bush, as he was about to leave the White House:

Farewell to you, George Herbert Walker.
Though never treasured as a talker—
Your predicates were always prone
To wander, nounless, off alone—
You did your best in your own way,
The way of Greenwich Country Day.
So just relax, and take your ease,
And never order Japanese.

Often, I've been snapped out of these reveries by some reminder that the man in charge is now the younger Bush, and that he may have inherited little from his father beyond a certain difficulty with the English language. Toward the end of George W. Bush's first term, I realized that I'd fallen into his habit of giving people nicknames. I had taken to calling the then national security advisor Mushroom Cloud Rice, a reference to her comment in the propaganda run-up to the Iraq war that "we don't want the smoking gun to be a mushroom cloud." Given the number of color-coded terrorism alerts called by the then attorney general, John Ashcroft, I'd begun to think of him as Orange John. I can still picture Orange John standing in the Great Hall of the Justice Department, where he had arranged to have the bare breast of the Spirit of Justice statue covered with a drape. In calling an orange alert, he would tell us, at one and the same time, that we were in mortal danger of being attacked and that we should go on about our usual business. I called the vice president Five Deferments Dick or, when I wanted to acknowledge his caregiver role in the White House, Nanny Dick.

In essence, "you're doing a heckuva job" is what Bush told Five Deferments Dick and the other architects of the Iraq debacle. Mushroom Cloud Rice was promoted to secretary of state. Paul Wolfowitz, who testified before the war that the Iraqis not only would greet us as liberators but also would pay for their own reconstruction, was made president of the World Bank, apparently for the financial acumen that allowed him to miscalculate the cost of the adventure to American taxpayers by only a couple hundred billion dollars. Donald Rumsfeld, whose insistence on invading Iraq with too few troops is now considered a central cause of the troubles that followed, was kept on for a second term, still conducting press conferences as if trying patiently to explain the obvious to a class of slow third graders. ("Might you prefer to be briefed by someone less arrogant and condescending? Yes. Do we always get what we want? Of course not.") L. Paul Bremer III, whose dismantling of the Iraqi army made him, in effect, the recruiting sergeant for the insurgency, was given the Medal of Freedom, as was George (Slam Dunk) Tenet. Nanny Dick Cheney was back for a second term, of course, as presumably the only vice president in the history of the republic to come to the defense of wiretapping without a warrant, indefinite imprisonment without the right to see a lawyer, and torture—all in the cause of spreading democracy.

I can imagine the whole flawless crew someday at a heckuva job reunion. There's the President, circling through the crowd with a pat on the back here and an encouraging word there. "Wolfie, you did a heckuva job," he says, and "Brems-babes, you did a heckuva job," and "Rummy, you did a heckuva job." Finally, the crowd hushes for his remarks, and he says simply, "All of us. We all did a heckuva job!"

part 1

Speaking of 9/11...

I CAN'T APPEAR WITHOUT MY NANNY DICK

(George W. Bush Explains the Interview Arrangements
He Has Made with the 9/11 Commission)

When called upon to testify,
I said I was a busy guy
So maybe we could do it on the phone.
They really want a face-to-face.
I said, OK, if that's the case,
I'm certainly not doing it alone.

I can't appear without my Nanny Dick.
For Nanny Dick I've got a serious jones.
I can't appear without my Nanny Dick.
I love the way he cocks his head and drones.

Cartoonists show me as a dummy,*
With voice by Cheney (or by Rummy).
I am the butt of every late-night satirist.
But I just can't go solitaire.
I need the help that's due an heir.
I need a dad, and Dad's a multilateralist.

I can't appear without my Nanny Dick.
He brings along a gravitas I lack.

* Though Charlie McCarthy's the dummy / Whose name has been most often
  heard, / Some folks who remember that act say / I'm closer to Mortimer Snerd.

I can't appear without my Nanny Dick—
The one who knows why we attacked Iraq.

Yes, Condi Rice is quite precise
With foreign policy advice
On who's Afghani and who's Pakistani.
I like to have her near in case
I just can't place some foreign face,
But Condoleezza Rice is not my nanny.

I can't appear without my Nanny Dick.
I wouldn't know which facts I should convey.
I can't appear without my Nanny Dick.
It's Nanny Dick who tells me what to say.

—APRIL 26, 2004

THE ONLY TIME GEORGE W. BUSH SEEMED RELUCtant to talk about 9/11 was when he was asked to appear before the 9/11 Commission. Otherwise, he mentioned it constantly, usually just before mentioning the importance of taking our fight against terrorism to Iraq. Considering his attempt to make his case by what rhetoricians might call relentless juxtaposition, George W. Bush may someday be referred to by historians as the Great Conflater.

At the 9/11 hearings, the President's team seemed like unnaturally shy actors pulled onstage for a curtain call. Orange John Ashcroft was there, denying that in the pre-9/11 period he'd told the FBI that he didn't want to be bothered with any more reports about terrorism threats. Mushroom Cloud Rice appeared, insisting that there was no "silver bullet" that might have prevented the attack. She seemed reluctant to reveal the title of the daily intelligence briefing delivered to the President at his Crawford ranch one morning in August 2001, before the full day of brush cutting and mountain biking and general summer fun began. The title was, she finally acknowledged, "Bin Laden Determined to Attack in the United States."

WE WERE READY

(Sung to the 9/11 Commission by the Bush Boys' Choir,
to the Tune of "I Feel Pretty" from *West Side Story*)

CHORUS:
We were ready—
Oh, so ready.
Sure, it happened, but those were the breaks.
And remember
That we never, ever make mistakes.

Sure, some mornings
Bush got warnings
To beware of some terror by air—
Just vague warnings,
And the numbers of the flights weren't there.

SOLO BY JOHN ASHCROFT:
Yes, that FBI guy did say that I
Wished terror reports left unsaid.
What a terrible lie!
From the FBI!
With my go-ahead,
God will strike him dead!

We were ready—
Oh, so ready.
To repulse any foreign assault.
So what happened
Really had to be Bill Clinton's fault.

—MAY 10, 2004

CONDOLEEZZA (MUSHROOM CLOUD) RICE EXPLAINS HER SILVER BULLET THEORY TO THE 9/11 COMMISSION

Because no silver bullet could have stopped
This horrifying deed from being done,
We cannot blame those dozing on the job
For never even loading up the gun.

—MAY 3, 2004

CONCERNING NANNY DICK CHENEY'S CONTINUED STATEMENTS ABOUT IRAQ'S ROLE IN 9/11

The Commission's report starts anew
Nanny's fairy tales, worthy of Pooh.
For the contrary facts that accrue
Can do nothing to change Cheney's view.
He believes, from what we can construe,
If you say it enough, then it's true.

—JULY 12, 2004

A WHITE HOUSE RESPONSE TO THE 9/11 COMMISSION'S FINDING THAT IRAN HAD MORE CONTACT WITH THE HIJACKERS THAN IRAQ DID

The little error that we may have made
In picking out a country to invade
Was understandable. The names, of course,
Are close, and when you make a show of force
The choice of countries needn't be clear-cut.
We simply had to kick some Muslim butt.

—AUGUST 16, 2004

and, eighteen months later...

A TRANSCRIPT: PHONE CONVERSATION BETWEEN THE 9/11 COMMISSION AND THE WHITE HOUSE CONCERNING THE COMMISSION'S BLISTERING REPORT CARD ON HOW WELL ITS RECOMMENDATIONS HAVE BEEN FOLLOWED

COMMISSION:
So firemen can talk to cops,
You must provide a frequency.
The fact that this has not been done
Is government delinquency.

WHITE HOUSE:
Iraq is coming right along.
We're confident we'll win this war.
The way to honor lads we've lost
Is stick it out (and lose some more).

COMMISSION:
Disaster funds are handed out
By pork, not risk, and, by the way,
The loose nukes that so worried us
Are getting looser every day.

WHITE HOUSE:

Our troops are making progress now,
And trained Iraqis have increased.
We win the battles that we fight.
We've taken some towns twice at least.

COMMISSION:

Still, airfreight cargo goes unchecked,
And information goes unshared.
We told you then, we tell you now:
The USA is unprepared!

WHITE HOUSE:

Saddam—that evil, awful man—
Is captured, living in a cell.
Democracy will spread from there.
The Middle East will soon be swell.

COMMISSION:

We have to say, upon reflection,
There's something wrong with this connection.

—DECEMBER 26, 2005

THAT FINAL REPORT of the 9/11 Commission was a bit scary, but I reassured myself by believing some things that terrorist experts didn't necessarily believe. For instance, I'm convinced that the whole shoe-bomber business was a prank. What got me onto this theory was reading that the shoe-bomber, a Muslim convert named Richard Reid, had been described by someone who knew him well in England as "very, very impressionable." I had already decided that the man was a complete bozo. He made such a goofy production of trying to light the fuses hanging off his shoe that he practically asked the flight attendant if she had a match. The way I figure it, the one terrorist in England with a sense of humor, a man known as Khalid the Droll, had said to the cell, "I bet I can get them all to take off their shoes in airports." So this prankster set up poor impressionable Reid and won his bet. Now Khalid is back there cackling at the thought of all those Americans exposing the holes in their socks on cold airport floors. If someone is arrested one of these days and is immediately, because of his M.O., referred to in the press as the underwear bomber, you'll know I was onto something.

part 2

The War in Nine Stanzas

1.

We chose, in this millennium's first test,
Between two lesser heirs, who, at their best,
If they'd been born as sons of other pops,
Might hope to be elected sheriff, tops.
(At school, Bush was a dunce, there's no denying.
Young Gore did not stand out—and *he* was trying.
A frat-house honcho, Bush reprised that part;
Young Gore portrayed a piece of chain saw art.)
In Florida, the fate of these two lads,
Appeared for days to hang on hanging chads.
'Twas Tilden-Hayes it put one in the mind of.
And then at last the Bush heir won, or kind of.

2.

When job and Wall Street numbers both declined,
The pundits in the capital opined,
"If Bush the Second doesn't watch his step, he
Is going to be a second one-term preppy."
And then, as many briefers had predicted,
Bin Laden and his terrorists inflicted
A mighty blow. With our own planes they smote us.
At first the President seemed not to notice:
While reading to a class, he didn't quit
When told the second tower had been hit.
Befuddlement was on his face writ large.
Then someone must have said, "Sir, you're in charge."

3.

Though nothing showed Iraq had played a part,
That's where some hawks thought vengeance ought to start.
(Then terrorists could count on what we'd do:
Attack us, we'll strike back, though not at you.)
We toppled first that band of Afghan loonies
Who'd let bin Laden hide out in their boonies.
The Taliban were smashed in one fell swoop.
Bin Laden, though, had plainly flown the coop.
Bush then forgot that name, and said, "In fact,
Iraq's the place that has to be attacked."
The war, Rove thought, with this one course correction,
Could still endure until the next election.

4.

Bush said that our security was based
On getting this Saddam erased posthaste.
In crimes, Saddam's CV was hardly lacking,
Though that was true when he'd enjoyed our backing.
But now he had these weapons we'd forbidden,
The White House said; we knew where they were hidden.
One saw Saddam Hussein, George Bush implied,
Behind that awful day our people died.
And therefore, Condoleezza Rice allowed,
The next attack might be a mushroom cloud.
Yes, Cheney, Rumsfeld, Colin Powell, too,
Said lots of things they had to know weren't true.

5.

"To war!" the neoconnish hawks all said.
(They'd nested in the space in Bush's head.)
Saddam was Hitler, circa '39,
They said. It's up to us to draw the line.
Though they'd been draft evaders to a man,
They talked as tough as cowpokes in Cheyenne.
Iraq will greet our boys and girls with petals,
Hawks said, and when the dust of warfare settles,
Iraq will pay the reconstruction bill,
And, one by one, the Arab countries will
Democratize as fast as they are able,
Like dominoes that snap up from the table.

6.

For us to fight to right what needed righting
Was right, they said, though others did the fighting.
As power for the good, we were exempt
From rules of war: The US could preempt.
Old allies who did not see things our way
Were soon dismissed as weasels or passé.
While making fun of duped U.N. inspectors,
Hawks brandished facts from Chalabi's defectors.
And so we conquered Baghdad and the rest,
As Bush would on a flight deck soon attest.
He wore his flight suit for that panorama—
The suit he hadn't used in Alabama.

7.

But what we'd set to righting went so wrong
It stirred some memories of the Vietcong.
Unduped inspectors came to realize
That Chalabi had fed us lies. Surprise!
There never was a flower-petal shower.
They saw us as an occupying power.
While we paid Cheney's cronies to rebuild,
Iraqis cheered to see our soldiers killed.
Insurgent forces and our troops still battled
As Jerry Bremer and his crew skedaddled.
For them Bush spun the spin that he could muster—
The sort of speech last used for praising Custer.

8.

With kidnappings and bombings on the rise,
Our partners started saying their goodbyes.
And even Colin Powell has now confessed
The coalition seems less coalesced.
The older allies we had roundly dissed
Declined our invitation to assist.
No domino's snapped up as hopeful token
The Middle East is fixed. It seems more broken—
More anti-US hatred than before,
More fresh recruits to fight a holy war.
In Europe, though, most people take the view
The danger's not from Muslims but Bush II.

9.

The weapons that we went to war to get
Have not, as Bush might say, been found just yet.
And even Bush no longer seeks to blame
Iraq for when the towers were aflame.
You needn't have clairvoyance to intuit
This war's against a man who didn't do it.
The man who did is laughing up his sleeve
As parents of our fallen soldiers grieve.
Although we live in color-coded dread,
This war has made us safer, Bush has said.
Most voters like the way he's fought the terror.
And Bush, when asked, could not recall one error.

—AUGUST 15, 2004

part 3

Don't Change Scaremongers in the Middle of the Stream

PLANNING THE REPUBLICAN NATIONAL CONVENTION seemed pretty simple: Get as close to Ground Zero as possible without having to hold the convention outdoors, and keep the wingnuts (also known as the leaders of the party's base) off of prime-time television.

The wacko right has mostly just disdain
For Schwarzenegger, Rudy, and McCain.
But they'll be featured at the prime-time mike
As just the sort of folks swing voters like.
The wackos then emerge from yonder ditch.
Consumer bureaus call this bait and switch.

Republicans who were concerned about a three-debate matchup between Yale debater John Kerry and Yale frat-house president George W. Bush had their worst fears realized in the first go-around. Bush seemed alternately peevish and bewildered. Although surveys indicated that Kerry "won" all three debates, the President's performance improved in the final two. I don't believe any newspaper used what seemed to me to be the obvious headline for the analysis piece on Bush's recovery in the later debates: PRESIDENT NOT COMPLETELY EMBARRASSING.

WHY DID THE PRESIDENT LOOK SO ANGRY?

Plain pleasantness has been his stock-in-trade.
From privilege, he'd cleverly remade
Himself into a NASCAR type of guy—
The sort of guy who's happy to supply
Cute nicknames, all bestowed with charm and grace.
So how come Bush had such an angry face?
On NBC or Fox or Time and Warner
He looked just like a kid sent to the corner—
Made petulant, with thoughts all dark and grim,
Like why the teacher always picked on him.
It's possible the President had sensed
This wasn't Gore whom he was up against.
Or saw his repetitions would betray
He hadn't really quite enough to say.
It's possible that he still thought it wrong
They hadn't let Dick Cheney come along.
Perhaps, behind those podiums they'd got,
His pants had gotten twisted in a knot.

—OCTOBER 1, 2004

A CLOSE FOLLOWER OF THE DEBATES COMES TO THE REALIZATION THAT GEORGE W. BUSH MAY STILL NOT KNOW THAT IRAQ HAD NO WEAPONS OF MASS DESTRUCTION

It seems bizarre, but these debates may show
That he's the only one who doesn't know.
Why else insist that sanctions couldn't have worked
And that the evil terrorists who lurked
Around those parts could get a germ or bomb
If we had not removed posthaste Saddam?
Bush wouldn't have learned the truth from news reports.
He's said he reads no papers. Maybe sports,
But otherwise his staff gives him the news,
And they, by now familiar with his views,
May, even as the facts came clear, have feared
To say his casus belli's disappeared.
The first debate revealed just how he acts
When he's confronted with unpleasant facts.
It's understandable they might feel terror
At telling someone who admits no error
There's evidence of one mistake he made
When he selected countries to invade.

—OCTOBER 9, 2004

33

SOMEONE WHO STILL WANTS TO KNOW WHETHER THE BULGE IN THE BACK OF GEORGE W. BUSH'S JACKET IN THE FIRST DEBATE WAS A RADIO TRANSMITTER TRIES TO CONCENTRATE ON THE FINAL DEBATE

The first time round a bulge was spotted 'neath his jacket—
A large, square bulge that blogs suspected was a packet
Transmitting info when the questions got too tough,
A high-tech way of writing answers on your cuff.
Could this explain his odd expressions? Is there proof he
Was being told "If you can hear me now, look goofy"?
Last night, I tried to listen to what he had to say,
But I kept wishing he would turn the other way
So I could ascertain if he had some receiver
Instructing him to smile as much as Beaver Cleaver.
Despite the third straight win John Kerry was compiling,
Our leader seemed determined he would keep on smiling.
The surveys show the President's now oh-for-three.
Yes, such a score might well discourage you and me,
So "Why is this man smiling?" is something we don't know—
Except, of course, he knows that Jesus loves him so.
And, also, in all schools that he was introduced to,
That oh-for-three reflects the sort of mark he's used to.

—OCTOBER 14, 2004

WATCHING DICK CHENEY IN DEBATE

I must say this, in studying Dick Cheney:
The man betrays no impulse to be zany,
Resembling in his scowl and condescendence
The stern vice principal who checks attendance.
He plants himself. In fact, I think it's fair
To say he seems stuck firmly to his chair.
He growls his answers in the sort of tone
You hear from bill collectors on the phone.
And when he tells a whopper, like denying
That he has gone around this land implying
Re 9/11 that Saddam's Iraq
Was mixed up in that awful sneak attack,
He seems so certain of his point of view
You almost think that what he's said is true.
At any time now, goes his favorite thesis,
Chicago could get blasted all to pieces.
So his look's hard enough for stones to glance off
As he drones on and tries to scare our pants off.

—OCTOBER 6, 2004

RATHER SURPRISINGLY, the Vietnam War, which had never been an issue in a presidential election campaign while it was being fought, became a campaign issue thirty years later. Karl Rove's Swift Boat Surrogates suggested that John Kerry had not deserved every single medal he got. George W. Bush ran into a replay of the old charges that he had been AWOL for a year while attached to the National Guard in Alabama. I was moved to come to the defense of Dan Quayle. In 1988, I reminded everybody, Quayle was set to be bounced from the ticket if it could be proved that the considerable influence of his family had been used to get him a safe berth in the National Guard. (Out of the more than 58,000 American servicemen who died in Vietnam, ninety-seven were Guardsmen—presumably people who, unlike George W. Bush, had checked the box indicating that they volunteered to go overseas.) In the controversy about Bush having been AWOL, nobody seriously contested the fact that family influence was used to skip him over five hundred people for a slot in the so-called Champagne Unit of the Texas Air National Guard. Was Dan Quayle being held to a higher standard not just on spelling but on military service? Or was this yet another example of what had become my nearly blind loyalty to members of the George H. W. Bush administration?

NOT WOUNDED ENOUGH

Republicans say Kerry might have got
Some wounds, but not the kind that hurt a lot.
Their own man cannot ever be accused
Of claiming wounds when he was only bruised:
He might have gotten banged up in that summer he
Was skipping all those meetings in Montgomery,
But slipping on some beer while chasing booty
Is not considered "in the line of duty."

—MAY 17, 2004

THE VIETNAM CONFESSIONS OF GEORGE W. BUSH

> *I am angry that so many sons of the powerful and well placed . . .*
> *managed to wangle slots in Reserve and National Guard units.*
> —Colin Powell on the Vietnam War, in *My American Journey*

With tentacles like wealthy octopi,
The well-connected didn't have to die.
The unit's full? We knew just what to do:
One made a call and simply jumped the queue.
Yes, keeping out of danger wasn't really hard.
I used my daddy's clout to hide out in the Guard.

Oppose the war? That seemed to me psychotic.
We Bushes, after all, are patriotic.
I backed the war. I wasn't disaffected.
I served,* but safely, being well-connected.
I partied right at home; my record was unmarred.
I used my daddy's clout to hide out in the Guard.

John Kerry's well-connected, as you know.
But, like a sucker, he signed up to go.
So, though I wear my flight suit and I primp,
His medals made me seem to be a wimp.

---

* Well, yes, I skipped about a year of meetings, / For which I've faced my only
kind of flak. / If you can find my records of that period, / Then you can find
those weapons in Iraq.

While he was in a boat that Charlie could bombard,
I used my daddy's clout to hide out in the Guard.

So Rove, sub rosa, managed to unchain,
The sort of creeps who vilified McCain.
With coverage that soon becomes intensive,
The valor's smudged, the hero turns defensive.
And voters soon forget why I emerged unscarred:
I used my daddy's clout to hide out in the Guard.

—SEPTEMBER 13, 2004

A SHORT HISTORY OF SOMEONE WHO FAILED TO GET INTO THE CHAMPAGNE UNIT OF THE TEXAS AIR NATIONAL GUARD IN 1968

I wasn't really for the war.
But all my kin, in wars before,
Had gone when called. I couldn't flee.
No, Canada was not for me.
Another thing that I was not
Was someone wanting to get shot.

I thought the Guard would be my out,
But Daddy didn't have the clout
To get me off the waiting list.
He knew no pol who might assist
In putting me above the rest.
With influence we were unblessed.

And movement in the list seemed dead,
As heirs of big shots shot ahead.
So I was called by Uncle Sam,
And made a grunt, and sent to 'Nam.
I wrote home once, said I was fine.
Then Charlie got me with a mine.

Historians may not recall
My name, now chiseled on that wall.
Still, they might say I played a role
By going on that last patrol
And not returning to my base:
I might have died in Bush's place.

—OCTOBER 4, 2004

I WOULD SUM UP the rest of the 2004 presidential election campaign this way: George W. Bush said one thing over and over again.
John Kerry said any number of things, most of them at length. The
one thing George W. Bush said over and over again was some com-
bination of the following: 9/11, Iraq, strength, war on terrorism,
and, for good measure, 9/11 again. Occasionally, he threw in the
word "evil," one of his favorite rhetorical weapons in the war on
terrorism. Discussing a post-9/11 program of the Small Business
Administration, the President had once said that grants would be
available to businesses in "areas impacted by the attacks from the
evil ones."

A POEM OF REPUBLICAN POPULISM

Our policies address the cares
Of heiresses and millionaires.
Our point of view reverberates
With folks who live behind high gates
And folks whose country clubs may lack
A single Jew, a single black.
We're backed by all the CEOs.
We waive the regs that bring them woes.
To comfort them is our intent.
Yes, though we always represent
The folks who sit in corporate boxes,
The gratifying paradox is—
And this we love; it's just the neatest—
The other party's called elitist.

—OCTOBER 11, 2004

WHY THE REPUBLICANS MIGHT BE RIGHT THAT
OSAMA BIN LADEN IS ROOTING FOR JOHN KERRY

Bin Laden is the name I bear,
And, modestly, I think it's fair
To say it's thought by spies and cops
Among all terrorists I'm tops.
And therefore it's a crying shame
This fellow Bush won't say my name.

At first he said it, like a curse:
He said that I'd be caught, or worse.
But when I vanished, his refrain
Became about Saddam Hussein.
Well, jihad's nice, but so's acclaim.
This fellow Bush won't say my name.

If Kerry wins, it's true that he
May concentrate his troops on me.
It's true that Bush's weird pursuits
Are means for me to get recruits.
But still, I must reclaim my fame.
This fellow Bush won't say my name.

—OCTOBER 18, 2004

A PRESIDENT WHO LISTENS TO A HIGHER AUTHORITY

He can't remember one mistake.
He'll stay on course 'til Hades freezes.
How can he be so certain still?
Because he's got the word from Jesus.

In meetings of his White House staff,
Unquestioning commitment pleases,
Since human doubts mean nothing to
A man who's got the word from Jesus.

He treats his critics in the press
As if they're yapping Pekineses.
Reporters deal in mundane facts;
This man has got the word from Jesus.

He can't believe that you'd support
The sort of man who eats French cheeses,
When you can vote to keep in place
A man who's got the word from Jesus.

—NOVEMBER 8, 2004

part 4

In the Court of George II, Cowboy Monarch

FAREWELL, COLIN POWELL

We need to say farewell to Colin Powell,
Who should have long ago tossed in the towel.
Instead he lent his good name to the team
In vouching for its plainly trumped-up scheme.
And now the team has shoved him out the door—
Not needed anymore (they got their war).
He's let himself be used by lesser men.
It's sad to see, as we remember when
Some thought he was the president-elect to be,
How easily is done a Colinectomy.

—DECEMBER 13, 2004

GIVEN THAT THE MOST DRAMATIC MOMENT OF COLIN Powell's tenure as secretary of state had been a United Nations speech vouching for the presence of weapons of mass destruction in Iraq, the public response to his ending decades of public service was not what it might have been four years before:

Instead of getting loud congrats, he
Was widely labeled as a patsy.

The other prominent cabinet member stepping down was Attorney General John Ashcroft—free now to roam the country protecting the bare breasts of statues from the prurient stares of degenerate statuephiliacs. (He decided instead to set up as a K Street lobbyist.) It wasn't until several months later that I realized we were no longer having orange alerts:

You know the things I miss so much it hurts?
Those orange alerts.
Routines, our leaders said—and this was strange—
Should not be changed:
If we stayed home, or stopped what we'd begun,
The bad guys won.
No, we were only told to be prepared
For being scared.

And when will it return—this orange protection?
The next election.

It has occurred to me that someday the government might celebrate some landmark in John Ashcroft's life by calling one more orange alert: At high noon, citizens everywhere would pay tribute to Orange John by, well, going on about their usual business.

ON THE APPOINTMENT OF ALBERTO
GONZALES AS ATTORNEY GENERAL

The AG's to be one Alberto Gonzales—
Dependable, actually loyal *über alles.*
Though we can't say "¡Viva!"
For him on Geneva
(Conventions he'd treat
As quite obsolete),
The fact he's not Ashcroft does bring us some solace.

—DECEMBER 6, 2004

ON THE REAPPOINTMENT OF JOHN SNOW
AS SECRETARY OF THE TREASURY

The people in the know said Snow
Was someone who would have to go.
The dollar's at an all-time low.
On Wall Street, numbers fail to grow.
And jobs have not begun to flow
Enough to help the average Joe.
The White House leakers weren't gung ho
On Snow. They called him just so-so—
A schmo who operates below
A level that is apropos

For one whose job it is to know
Just how to make the markets glow.
But as Snow packed his portmanteau,
The White House said he'd undergo
A second four-year term. Although
It might be nice to help our dough
And mitigate the debt we owe
And take the market to, not fro,
Big changes we will now forgo.
It's loyalty Snow has to show.
Snow says he thinks, like Bush & Co.,
That taxing rich folks is *de trop.*
Unlike O'Neill, he won't say no
To economic schemes they throw
His way. He's Bush's fiscal ho.
So maybe we'll see Bush bestow,
In one more night-is-day tableau,
A Freedom Medal on John Snow.

—JANUARY 10, 2005

ASSIGNING RESPONSIBILITY

Defending Rumsfeld, Bush says Rummy's great,
That as a planner he has been first-rate—
Respected in the White House and the ranks.
The same is true, of course, of Tommy Franks,
For he and Tenet and, yes, Bremer, too,
Got medals as they bid their jobs adieu.
And Bush, whose orders all these men obeyed,
Can't think of one mistake he might have made.
So everyone involved's a crackerjack.
The mess that made itself is in Iraq.

—JANUARY 25, 2005

CONDOLEEZZA RICE

(Sung to the Tune of "March of the Siamese Children" from *The King and I,* and Accompanied by the Secretary Herself on the Baby Grand)

Condoleezza Rice, who is cold as ice, is precise with her advice.
> Yes, she is quite precise, and, yes, she's cold as ice.

In her can be found talents that abound. She's renowned, though
> tightly wound. Yes, talents can be found, and, yes, she's
> tightly wound.

She once avowed we might see a large mushroom cloud if more
> reign by Hussein were allowed,

Which turned out to be: total bushwa, yes, total bushwa.

When she accused him of buying tubes only used to make nukes
> the truth was abused.

And she knew she spoke total bushwa, yes, total bushwa.

So to serve her guy, she will testify to a lie she hopes you'll buy—
> to try to petrify, precisely tell a lie.

Condoleezza Rice, who is cold as ice, is precise with her advice.
> Yes, she is quite precise, and, yes, she's cold as ice.

—MARCH 7, 2005

ON THE REVELATION THAT DICK CHENEY REQUIRES THE TELEVISION TO BE PRESET TO FOX NEWS IN ANY HOTEL ROOM HE IS ABOUT TO OCCUPY

The networks give Bush knocks or mocks.
They paint him stubborn as an ox
And clever as a box of rocks.
So set the channel, please, to Fox.

Some commentators on the box
Like making us the laughingstocks.
Upon foul PBS a pox!
Just set the channel, please, to Fox.

That CNN will broadcast crocks
On Arabs managing our docks
And deaths in wars and other shocks.
Now set the channel, please, to Fox.

For me, the news that really rocks
Confirms beliefs held by our flocks.
My mind remains quite closed, with locks.
So set the channel, please, to Fox.

—APRIL 17, 2006

part 5

So Many Foxes in the Chicken Coop There's Hardly Room for the Chickens

I SOMETIMES WONDER WHAT WOULD HAVE HAPPENED if the Texas Rangers, the baseball team that George W. Bush helped run before he became governor, had used the same approach to signing players that President George W. Bush used when he, say, put a particularly aggressive lobbyist for the timber industry in charge of protecting our forests or named a coal company lobbyist to oversee mine safety regulations. At the Rangers press conference, the beaming general manager would announce the signing of a curveballer who is philosophically opposed to pitching within the strike zone. Among the governmental equivalents of anti-strike-zone curveballers was John Bolton; he was nominated to be American ambassador to the United Nations, an institution for which he had long expressed contempt. Even some of Bolton's political allies said he was known for intemperate outbursts aimed at people not in a position to return the fire. It occurred to me that Bush—whose impact internationally was descending toward negligible, unless you happened to live in a country he seemed about to invade—had not quite grasped a phrase associated with Theodore Roosevelt:

To send the UN Bolton shows that Bush
Has not grasped T.R.'s famous dictum fully.
Yes, Roosevelt has been misunderstood.
Bush lost the pulpit; he just has the bully.

BOLTON CHASES FRENCH AMBASSADOR UP TREE
(A Headline in the Future of John Bolton as American Ambassador to the United Nations)

The Frenchman voted wrong, in Bolton's mind—
Against a war. He doubted we would find
These weapons just where Bolton said they were,
Despite the fact that Bolton seemed so sure.
As Bolton shouted that the French were yellow,
His face took on the shade of cherry Jell-O.
The Frenchman thought it prudent then to flee,
And that's when Bolton chased him up a tree.
"How dare you!" Bolton shouted from below,
As with his shoe he struck the trunk a blow.
The French ambassador was plainly scared.
He kept repeating "Zut alors!" and "Merde!"
The White House, backing Bolton, said that he'll
Continue putting forth our case with zeal.

—JUNE 13, 2005

WHITE HOUSE SAYS BOLTON CAN CONTINUE TO DO THE JOB EVEN WHILE IN STRAITJACKET

(Another Headline in the Future of John Bolton as American Ambassador to the United Nations)

Twelve delegates were there but couldn't swear
Just why John Bolton chose to throw the chair,
Or why his face turned orange, then turned red,
Then turned a sort of Dubonnet instead.
They couldn't guess just why it might have been
That spittle came to cascade down his chin,
And noises came—a rumble, then a squeal,
And then a bark that sounded like a seal.
(The UK delegate was heard to mutter,
"Cor blimey, lads, I fear the man's a nutter.")
They couldn't say at all just what he shouted.
Interpreters who testified all doubted
The words were from a language that they knew—
Although they'd all decided to skiddoo,
And so they couldn't say they'd been around
When guards pinned Bolton, screaming, to the ground.
So even now it's not been ascertained
Why Bolton flipped and had to be restrained.
The White House had no comment on the trigger,
But said John Bolton pleads our case with vigor.

—JUNE 20, 2005

HARRIET MIERS, Bush's first choice to fill the seat being vacated by Sandra Day O'Connor, could not be accused of being philosophically opposed to the Supreme Court, but she was accused of almost everything else, from mediocre lawyering to unfortunate eyeliner. The President, who consistently referred to her as "Harriet" in announcing her nomination, presumably admired her loyalty, and, since I prize loyalty myself, I sometimes felt like giving her a cheer for that:

Who's willing to draw water for George Bush and carry it?
Harriet.
Who worked to take his DWI rap and bury it?
Harriet.
Who thinks anyone critical of him is Judas Iscariot?
Still Harriet.
Rah! Rah! Rah!

TROUBLE ON THE RIGHT

The President, who never tires
Of naming cronies, named Ms. Miers
To be a justice. I'm not kidding.
He said he knows she'll do his bidding.
The social-issues Right went crazy.
They called her record much too hazy.
Though through the code, with some contortion,
Bush signaled that she hates abortion,
They asked, so why is she not willing
To say right out it's baby killing?
Responding to this strong attack, he
Assured the Right she's really wacky.
In phone calls, Rove, in hopes of winning
Support from preachers gave this spinning:
It's by her church that ye shall know her.
Her church is low. No church is lower.
Her church friends (please think Holy Rollers)
Treat embryos like kids in strollers—
Including embryos of rapists.
The Baptists to these folks are papists.
She's not the moderate you deem her.
If you're extreme, then she's extremer.
Her style is not to be dramatic,
But be assured she is fanatic.

—OCTOBER 31, 2005

ONE POSSIBLE SCENARIO

The gang of right-wing-dogma verifiers
Continues in its dissing of Ms. Miers,
And hints her views don't differ much from Breyer's.
The intellectual Right says George Bush hires
Just hacks who act as ego fortifiers.
Then Bush, attacking all of his decriers,
Calls whinging neocons, in Yiddish, *schreiers,*
And then calls Will and Brooks and Kristol liars.
So they call him a dope—no qualifiers.
O'Connor reconsiders, unretires.

—NOVEMBER 7, 2005

part 6

Bringing Democracy, or Whatever, to Iraq

HUNKY-DORY IN IRAQ

(A Song Sung in the Shower Every Morning by George W. Bush)

It's all just hunky-dory in Iraq.

Yes, thanks to us, they've got their country back.

We showed the folks who thought our nerve would crack

And folks who were reluctant to attack—

Those girly men like Schroeder and Chirac.

Yes, things are hunky-dory in Iraq.

La-dee-dah.

La-dee-dah.

La-dee-dah.

—JANUARY 31, 2005

LTHOUGH THE SITUATION IN IRAQ NEVER SEEMED to change, the backdrops for the President's speeches on Iraq did. The most famous, of course, was the huge MISSION ACCOMPLISHED banner on the deck of the carrier U.S.S. *Abraham Lincoln,* in the spring of 2003, when Bush said that major hostilities in Iraq were at an end (at that point, there had been 140 American fatalities). In a 2005 speech at the Naval Academy, in the face of sagging public support for the war, the President used the word "victory" fifteen times in front of a PLAN FOR VICTORY backdrop that looked as if it had been designed by someone who ordinarily does sets for product launches (PLAN FOR VICTORY AGAINST PLAQUE). A few days later, *The New York Times* revealed that the entire exercise had been concocted on the basis of a new White House consultant's surveys indicating that Americans will stand for casualties as long as the prospect of victory is present. I found myself awaiting the next backdrop. In one of those warehouses where the Pentagon keeps Vietnam War stuff, they must have one that says LIGHT AT THE END OF THE TUNNEL.

ON THE ABUSE OF PRISONERS IN IRAQ

We're told that the few rotten apples
Who brought on this sordid affair'll
Be punished. But what if those apples
Are right at the top of the barrel?

—MAY 31, 2004

THE COALITION AUTHORITY EXPLAINS
DEMOCRACY TO THE IRAQI PEOPLE

We'll give you back the country soon.
Your leaders at the end of June
Will be there democratically.
We'll let you know soon who they'll be.

Democracy is on the way.
We smashed this place to free it.
Democracy is on the way.
You'll know it when you see it.

Your press is free forever, but
The papers we were forced to shut
Should know, when all is said and done,
It's free, though not for everyone.

Democracy is on the way.
We smashed this place to free it.
Democracy is on the way.
You'll know it when you see it.

A person's treatment post-arrest
Can be democracy's true test—
Though, sometimes, soldiers are unkind,
Because . . . that is . . . oh, never mind.

Democracy is on the way.
We smashed this place to free it.
Democracy is on the way.
You'll know it when you see it.

—JUNE 7, 2004

THE NEOCONS CLUNG to Ahmed Chalabi, the convicted bank swindler whose phony intelligence on weapons of mass destruction they'd retailed to justify their war, almost as strongly as they clung to their Reverse Domino Theory. At the beginning of the war, they'd had the Pentagon fly Chalabi to Baghdad, confident that this émigré who had last set foot in Iraq during the Eisenhower administration and had no discernible support there would become the country's leader by acclamation. Eventually, American troops raided Chalabi's house because he was suspected of spying for the Iranians. But Chalabi had a con man's resilience. As a deputy prime minister a year and a half later, he was received in Washington by both Dick Cheney and Condoleezza Rice. When he ran with a slate of candidates for Iraq's 275-member parliament, in December 2005, his party won less than half of one percent of the vote and not a single seat.

ON THE RUPTURE OF RELATIONS BETWEEN AHMED CHALABI AND THE UNITED STATES OF AMERICA

The learned Wolfowitz and Perle, it seems,
Made Chalabi the hero of their dreams.
Yes, all the sissy hawks were glad to sup
On plainly foolish tales that he served up.
In triumph back in Baghdad he would pose—
A Charles de Gaulle, with more expensive clothes.
When Ahmed's hopes for power took a dive,
He thought he'd turn against us to survive.
We trashed his house, and now the man is vexed.
Pray tell: Will Wolfowitz's house be next?

—JUNE 14, 2004

GEORGE W. BUSH, THE LION OF BAGHDAD, DEMANDS THAT SYRIA WITHDRAW FROM LEBANON

You must withdraw, since nations can't
Install their troops in other places
To change regimes that they don't like.
Except, of course, in certain cases.

—APRIL 4, 2005

CHENEY SAYS IRAQI INSURGENTS ARE IN FINAL THROES

Dick's always sure. He knows what warfare is—
Enough to know it's not for him or his.
Insurgents somehow, though they're in the throes,
Kill more GIs—but no one Cheney knows.

—JULY 4, 2005

PENTAGON SECRETLY PAYING TO PLACE ARTICLES IN IRAQI NEWSPAPERS: ANOTHER LESSON IN DEMOCRACY

Democracy's the only way.
That's what we're giving U.S. aid for.
It's great to have a press that's free,
But better if it's bought and paid for.

—JANUARY 2, 2006

CHENEY, SPEAKING FROM EXPERIENCE

When shells fall close and smoke is thick,
Real tough guys never run. They stick.
Or so says Five Deferments Dick.

No wavering—no, he's a brick.
To cut and run would make him sick.
Or so says Five Deferments Dick.

Appeasers cannot take a lick,
But tough guys bite and gouge and kick.
Or so says Five Deferments Dick.

—DECEMBER 12, 2005

A SUMMARY OF REMARKS BY GEORGE W. BUSH
AND DICK CHENEY ON THE THIRD ANNIVERSARY
OF THE INVASION OF IRAQ

Our strategy for peace there
Is really working well.
It's just that all the killing
Can make that hard to tell.

—APRIL 10, 2006

part 7

A Plague in
Both Their Houses

H AD THE MAJORITY LEADERS OF BOTH HOUSES of Congress ever before been under investigation at the same time?

Investigators who persist
On looking at DeLay and Frist
Resist requests that they desist.
Which leader will be first dismissed?

That turned out to be Tom DeLay, a man who never met a rule he didn't try to slither out of. After being indicted by Ronnie Earle, the district attorney of Travis County, Texas, DeLay stepped down from his leadership post and eventually announced he was leaving the House. In the Senate, Majority Leader Bill Frist, who had both Princeton and Harvard to live down, furiously tried to shore up his support among the Christian Right for a presidential race in 2008; in his attempt to exploit the comatose Terri Schiavo, though, he couldn't keep up with a man who was then seen as a potential rival for the nomination, Jeb Bush, perhaps the only working ghoul ever to inhabit the governor's mansion in Tallahassee. Soon, the SEC was investigating Frist because he had ordered his "blind trust" to dump stock in his family's hospital business just before the stock tumbled. Although DeLay's downfall seemed to have no impact on the alliance between K Street and congressional Republicans, the guilty plea of kleptolobbyist Jack Abramoff caused the entire leadership to talk passionately of reform for several days.

I THINK I HEARD A LIBERAL SAY

I think I heard a liberal say
To Ronnie Earle, "Hooray! Hooray!
Because you finally made my day
When you indicted Tom DeLay.
They'll never fashion, come what may,
An ethics rule that he'd obey.
Corruption's in his DNA.
It dominates his résumé.
He works the shadowed shades of gray.
The moment that his side held sway,
He made the lobbyists on K
Just hire those who thought his way,
Then pay and pay and pay and pay.
For access, he did pay-to-play.
The Congress of the USA
Became the cages of Bombay.
So here's what I'd like for The Hammer:
A whole bunch of years in the slammer."

—DECEMBER 27, 2004

SENATOR BILL FRIST, A THORACIC SURGEON WHO MADE A NEUROLOGICAL DIAGNOSIS OF TERRI SCHIAVO AFTER WATCHING A VIDEO OF HER, REPORTS ON A PHYSICAL EXAMINATION HE'S DONE OF JEB BUSH, A POTENTIAL RIVAL FOR THE 2008 REPUBLICAN PRESIDENTIAL NOMINATION, AFTER OBSERVING ONE OF THE GOVERNOR'S FLORIDA PRESS CONFERENCES ON TELEVISION

From that slight slump I'd make the diagnosis
Of just a tiny touch of scoliosis,
Which likely could be kept in check unless
He tried to take a job with too much stress.
And judging from his pudginess of chops, he
Is likely to be suffering from dropsy.
From bagginess of trouser legs we see
He's got himself a case of housemaid's knee.
He could have gout, and judging from that pout,
There's serious PMS we can't rule out.
In time, this patient could be really fine,
If he just rests until at least '09.

—APRIL 18, 2005

ANOTHER MIRACLE FROM BILL FRIST

*(Wherein the doctor who proved himself a master of distance
diagnosis in the Terri Schiavo case offers a succinct explanation of
why he ordered his "totally blind" trust to dump his holdings in the
family health care company just before the stock dropped.)*

I followed rules on conflict with such care
That I sold stock I didn't know was there.

*(Whereupon his blind trust is examined by some law professors
with ophthalmological training.)*

This patient's sight shows some improvement,
Detecting shapes of market movement.

—NOVEMBER 14, 2005

A CONSIDERED JURISPRUDENTIAL ANALYSIS OF THE GUILTY PLEA BY YET ANOTHER FORMER AIDE TO TOM DeLAY AND DeLAY'S RESIGNATION ANNOUNCEMENT THREE DAYS LATER

This latest guilty plea, by Tony Rudy,
Convinced Tom he was stuck in deepest doody.

—APRIL 24, 2006

A MEMBER OF CONGRESS TRIES TO RECALL JACK ABRAMOFF

Uh, yeah, his restaurant was near.
I'd have a meal. I'd have a beer,
And shoot the breeze. I don't know why:
I really hardly knew the guy.

Well, yes, perhaps, I think I might
Have gone to see a game one night
With him, but I can testify
I really hardly knew the guy.

Oh, yeah, when campaign funds were low,
He'd hold events to raise some dough.
Though it's his box we'd occupy,
I really hardly knew the guy.

For golf in Scotland? Yeah, that's so.
When he arranged a trip, I'd go—
Just golfing. Nothing seemed awry.
I really hardly knew the guy.

Of course there was no quid pro quo!
Coincidence is what you'd show
If what he wanted got my aye.
I really hardly knew the guy.

—JANUARY 30, 2006

ON ROY BLUNT'S PROMISE TO REFORM LOBBYING RULES IF HE BECOMES HOUSE MAJORITY LEADER

I must be blunt where Blunt's concerned:
In service to DeLay he earned
His K Street Brownie points with clusters
For calling lobbyists to musters
Where bills were molded to a tee
By K Street and the GOP.
Yes, money poured from K Street tills
So lobbyists could write these bills.
Reformer's what they call this guy?
Then I'm the Sultan of Brunei.

—FEBRUARY 13, 2006

BUT BLUNT WAS DEFEATED by John Boehner, a newly converted reformer who had once been spotted distributing lobbyist checks to fellow congressmen on the floor of the House.

> He'd handed out checks on the floor
> Of Congress. (Yes, money galore
> From cigarette interests who thought
> That congressmen ought to be bought.)
> He says that this custom offended
> Some folks and he's glad that it's ended.
> He promises not to revive it.
> He'll hand out the money in private.

part 8

Secrets:
Keeping Them,
Leaking Them,
Extracting Them, and
Listening In on Them

BUSH ADMINISTRATION PRIORITIES ON NATIONAL SECRETS

When piqued at Ambassador Wilson,
The Bushmen saw no reason why
They shouldn't just leak to all quarters
The name of a CIA spy.

And Chalabi, Man from Armani,
Got secrets from them, whereupon
He called an Iranian pal up
And saw to it they were passed on.

But one of our secrets is safe still,
And access is tightly controlled:
The names on that energy task force.
That secret will never be told.

—JULY 5, 2004

SOMETIMES, TRYING TO CHEER MYSELF UP ON A GRAY day, I think of Dick Cheney being snatched off the streets of Washington by a black-op squad from the Sierra Club, "rendered" to some client country that is not overly concerned with the niceties, and there threatened with what even Alberto Gonzales would define as torture unless the membership list of the White House's energy task force is produced forthwith. Of course, the Administration insisted that it did not send prisoners to other countries to be tortured—expecting, perhaps, to leave the impression that the destinations were chosen according to the national cuisine or the sort of scenery visible from a dungeon window.

With a special prosecutor investigating the outing of Joseph Wilson's wife, Valerie Plame, as a CIA operative, George W. Bush spoke sternly against leaks of our own secrets—classified information— and said, "If there's a leak out of my administration, I want to know who it is." It took about two years for Bush to find out. Then it was revealed, in court papers filed by the prosecutors, that Cheney's former chief of staff, Scooter Libby, said he'd been told by Cheney that authorization to leak selectively from a highly classified National Intelligence Estimate had come from none other than President George W. Bush. There was a temptation to quote what may have been inscribed on the Delphic temple of the god Apollo, KNOW THYSELF, or what was definitely inscribed in the comic strip *Pogo:* "We have met the enemy and he is us."

ANOTHER LESSON FROM THE WHITE HOUSE OF VALUES

We stand up for values. Here's what we believe:
Gay marriage is something we just can't conceive
Of happening ever. The thought causes dread.
Gay men should just marry nice women instead.
If some of them marry not women but chaps,
Our civilization would simply collapse.
Abortion is murder. If we had our druthers,
We'd jail docs who do it, and also the mothers.
And research on stem cells is evil, a sin,
And so is bad language, and flicks that show skin.
And families other than these God forbids:
A dad and a mom and two point three kids.
And we support Jesus, and, oh, by the way,
When we think it's needed, some torture's OK.

—NOVEMBER 28, 2005

ON THE SECRET "RENDITION" OF TERROR SUSPECTS TO COUNTRIES KNOWN TO USE TORTURE

As Jesus said to render unto Caesar
A portion of thy grain or of thy stock,
Our policy's to render unto Caesar
In hopes that he'll apply electric shock.

—MARCH 28, 2005

KARL ROVE CONTEMPLATES FINE DISTINCTIONS

If somebody committed a crime, they will no longer work in my administration.
—George W. Bush

Ann Richards wasn't hard to beat—
Not once we said she seemed to greet
A lot of girls who looked quite burly
And, all and all, just not too girly.

We smear, we smear. We slime, we slime.
It's fine if it is not a crime.

McCain, a hero, led the pack,
Until our whispered sneak attack
Said, "Hero, sure, but he was changed
By prison. John is quite deranged."

We smear, we smear. We slime, we slime.
It's fine if it is not a crime.

Though our guy'd hidden in the Guard,
John Kerry, hero, soon was tarred
By swift-boat proxies who'd exact
A fearful price without one fact.

We smear, we smear. We slime, we slime.
It's fine if it is not a crime.

Joe Wilson's op-ed piece implied
When we lacked facts we simply lied.
We showed our toughness in this strife:
When he struck us, we smeared his wife.

We smear, we smear. We slime, we slime.
It's fine if it is not a crime.

—AUGUST 15, 2005

A REPUBLICAN NURSERY RHYME

Scooter Libby told a fib. He
Shouldn't have told at all.
Though not slimy all the time, he
Has to take the fall.

Permaslimer all-the-timer
Rove has got away.
Naught to plea to, he's now free to
Slime another day.

—NOVEMBER 21, 2005

A WHITE HOUSE RESPONSE TO SENATOR FEINGOLD

*The President believes he has the right to overrule laws the
Congress has passed. He is a president, not a king.*
—Senator Russell Feingold

As long as I'm in charge, Russ,
I'll spy on those who merit it.
If this is not a throne, Russ,
Just how did I inherit it?

—JANUARY 9, 2006

THE PRESIDENT'S MEASURED RESPONSE TO CRITICISM OF HIS SECRET DOMESTIC SPYING OPERATION

Since I am commander in chief,
My powers to spy or debrief
Are limitless. That's my belief.
So go somewhere else with your beef.
I'll do what I want when I want to.

Since terror is not like croquet,
The NSA does what I say.
Despite your softheaded dismay,

My Nanny Dick says it's OK.
I'll do what I want when I want to.

Security trumps, that's for sure.
And I get to say who's secure.
And laws and court warrants obscure
My mission. And I will endure!
I'll do what I want when I want to.

—JANUARY 23, 2006

GEORGE BUSH EXPLAINS THE "SIGNING STATEMENT" ISSUED WHEN HE SIGNED JOHN McCAIN'S ANTI-TORTURE AMENDMENT INTO LAW

> *The statement said that the administration would interpret the amendment "in a manner consistent with the constitutional authority of the president to supervise the unitary executive branch and as commander in chief and consistent with the constitutional limitations on judicial power."*
> —*The New York Times,* January 16, 2006

Since I'm the one in charge in war,
I'll do what I have done before
If it's consistent with my duties.

Is that an out? You bet your booties.
The boss is boss; he can't be bossed.
I signed, but with my fingers crossed.

We do not torture, never will.
So why did we oppose John's bill?
Don't ask, or you'll be in a van
And rendered to Uzbekistan.
McCain won't win. We haven't lost.
I signed, but with my fingers crossed.

—FEBRUARY 6, 2006

GEORGE W. BUSH'S APPROACH TO MAINTAINING CONSTITUTIONAL RULE IN A DEMOCRACY THROUGH A SERIES OF CHECKS AND BALANCES

On wiretaps, the war, and now Dubai,
He's sounded more and more like Captain Bligh.

—APRIL 3, 2006

part 9

Two Crooners Deny Having Misled the Country into War

PARTLY BECAUSE OF THE CRIMINAL INQUIRY INTO the Valerie Plame leak, questions about whether the country had been misled into war resurfaced in 2005. A leaked memo, written by the British note-taker at a Washington meeting months before the war, revealed that Bush's policy had been to remove Saddam by force and that "intelligence and facts were being fixed around the policy." An article in *Foreign Affairs* by Paul Pillar, who had been the intelligence officer for the Near East during the buildup to war, said, "The Administration used intelligence not to inform decision-making, but to justify a decision already made." According to George W. Bush, the Great Conflater, people who claimed that the Administration had misled the American people into war were giving comfort to the enemy. Nanny Dick Cheney—who to this day seems loath to abandon the notion that Mohammed Atta and Iraqi secret agents were spotted eating chicken paprikash together in Prague—said talk of the country's having been misled was "reprehensible."

DON'T CRITICIZE ME

(A ballad to the Tune of "You Go to My Head," Crooned by George W. Bush with Backup by Karl Rove and His Singing Slimemeisters)

Don't criticize me. 'Cause that's just the thing our enemies want.
And it damages our terrorist hunt,
And endangers every grunt at the front.

Yes, Cheney did swear that the weapons were there, but big deal—
Cheney's zeal's his appeal.
And don't say aloud Condi's next mushroom cloud was unreal.
We're sure she'll have more to reveal.

Don't criticize me. Evil foes would welcome that kind of strife.
Since their goal is crushing our way of life,
We might have to smear both you and your wife.
Don't criticize me.
Don't criticize me.

—DECEMBER 5, 2005

REPREHENSIBLE

(Sung to the Tune of "Unforgettable," That Old Nat King Cole Favorite,
by Dick Liar-Liar-Your-Pants-Are-On-Fire Cheney)

Reprehensible—that word is for
Charges we misled our folks to war.
Like, despite the facts, I'd demagogue
Atta's meeting with Iraq in Prague.
It still may have been. The facts are not in.

Reprehensible. It's just a crime
Saying that a liar is what I'm.
Like we talked of mushroom clouds to come
From the tubes made of aluminum,
For all that we knew, it might have been true.

Reprehensible! I'm just appalled
At the sort of names we're being called.
Like we'd say they'd bought some yellowcake
Even when we knew that tale was fake.
Catching us is reprehensible too.

—DECEMBER 19, 2005

part 10

The Emperor Has Cowboy Boots, but Otherwise No Clothes

GEORGE W. BUSH'S APPROVAL RATING SINKS TO 34 PERCENT

Most pols would find another path to take
Or look for policies they might forsake,
For those are numbers they could not abide.
But those pols don't have Jesus on their side.

—MARCH 27, 2006

VEN BEFORE THE PRESIDENT DEMONSTRATED THAT the near destruction of one of the nation's principal cities was not sufficient reason to interrupt good times on the ranch, he was losing ground. The centerpieces of his domestic and foreign affairs agenda—Social Security privatization and the war in Iraq—had become almost equally unpopular. Gas prices were up. Mainstream voters had been repulsed by White House interference in the Terri Schiavo case. And when Pat Robertson put a sort of Low Church *fatwa* on Hugo Chavez of Venezuela or said that Ariel Sharon had been visited with a stroke for dividing God's land, Bush was hardly in a position to say, "Could there really be mullahs loonier than this?"

> *I owe him much: He smeared McCain when my campaign was*
> *   almost toast.*
> *The wacko crowd that follows him we call our base; I need them*
> *   most.*
> *So criticizing Pat by me is something that will not be done.*
> *I am, when all is said and done, a Robertson Republican.*

As the President's approval rating began to slide, he made what was for him a breathtaking act of contrition. He began acknowledging that not everything in the Iraq war had gone according to plan— not surprising, since it had become increasingly clear that there hadn't really been a plan for everything to go according to.

GEORGE W. BUSH, WHO SAYS HE'S A MAN WITH A LOT OF POLITICAL CAPITAL, FINDS THAT HE HAS NO LIQUIDITY

He's lost support and stirred up people's fears
With plans to fiddle with their golden years.
Iraq's a mess, and, everyone agrees,
Schiavo exploitation failed to please
The folks who thought our way of life forbore us
From meddling in other people's *tsoris.*
With gas too dear to start a truck up,
His only answer is some Saudi suck-up.
DeLay, it's clear, is wallowing in graft,
And Bolton seems at least a little daft.
(Forgiveness, Khrushchev, surely is your due
If our guy starts to rant and pound his shoe.)
So Bush's numbers tumble toward the floor,
Reminding us of what we've seen before.
But why is that? Why does this path seem trodden?
Remember what Bush was before bin Laden.

—MAY 23, 2005

A PRESIDENTIAL EXPLANATION OF PATRIOTIC LOAFING

If terror changes what you've always done,
Well, then, the terrorists have really won.
Right now, when vicious terrorism's rife,
It's vital to maintain a balanced life.
So live your whole life now, not just a fraction—
Unless, of course, you've just been killed in action.

—SEPTEMBER 12, 2005

FURTHER WORDS FROM GEORGE W. BUSH AFTER HE SAID TO FEMA CHIEF MICHAEL BROWN, "BROWNIE, YOU'RE DOING A HECKUVA JOB."

A qualified guy, I wish I had added.
Your résumé's super, even if padded.
We wanted the best to lead FEMA's forces,
And who would know more than a man who knows horses?
You saw that the storm was more than some showers,
And sent off a memo in four or five hours.
You found out that life in the Dome was not Super—
And only a day after Anderson Cooper.
A heckuva job! You know how to lead 'em.
We hope to award you the Medal of Freedom.

—OCTOBER 3, 2005

A NEW GILBERT AND SULLIVAN SONG ABOUT
GEORGE W. BUSH AS A TAKE-CHARGE GUY

I keep my slicker by my bed, and, sure, my bullmike's handy too.
With these, it looks as if I've got the slightest notion what to do.
On Air Force One my staff and I will fly to every storm we're
    fighting.
My staff's prepared. They've studied film. They've got technique.
    They know backlighting.
You'll soon forget the FEMA hacks appointed, one and all, by me.
A leader is a man who finds a photo opportunity.

CHORUS:
No matter what, there'll always be a photo opportunity.
And otherwise, I'm always free for loafing with impunity.
Because, you see, we all agree: With Karl there to fine-tune it, he
Can find a way to picture me at one with the community.
No matter what, there'll always be a photo opportunity.

So clueless had I seemed before—for days when that Katrina hit—
I have to show some leadership: This slicker is a perfect fit.
No way that I'd be in the way, the way the coverage implied.
To get the shot, we've never pushed one rescue worker to the side.
So, clueless still, you say, but watch: This not how folks will
    picture me,
For now each storm will be for me a photo opportunity.

No matter what, there'll always be a photo opportunity.
And otherwise, I'm always free for loafing with impunity.
Because, you see, we all agree: With Karl there to fine-tune it, he
Can find a way to picture me at one with the community.
No matter what, there'll always be a photo opportunity.

—OCTOBER 17, 2005

GOVERNMENT'S THE PROBLEM

(A Chorus from the Bush Administration Sings Another Republican
Sea Chantey)

We weren't impressed with FEMA when we came—
Too set on fitting jobs to skills precisely.
It's loyalty we needed at the top.
We thought a horse show judge could do quite nicely.

'Cause government's the problem, lads.
Americans would all do well to shun it.
Yes, government's the problem, lads.
At least it is when we're the ones who run it.

And why should we have rushed in troops to help?
These people seem to think that they're our clients.
They're not. They got a little wet. So what?
America was built on self-reliance.

'Cause government's the problem, lads.
Americans would all do well to shun it.
Yes, government's the problem, lads.
At least it is when we're the ones who run it.

—OCTOBER 10, 2005

GOVERNMENT'S THE PROBLEM (REPRISE)

(Another Verse of the Republican Sea Chantey, Again Sung by the
Bush Administration's Famed All-Thumbs Chorale)

Some seniors say they're baffled by
Our drug plan, and we won't deny
It's complicated. That's too bad,
But complications simply had
To be included in this plan:
We promised donors when we ran
That we'd enrich with every claim
Our pals in the insurance game.
If they don't get their cut, you see
It's socialistic as can be—
Like Medicare, which we've surmised
Should certainly be privatized.

'Cause government's the problem, lads.
Americans would all do well to shun it.
Yes, government's the problem, lads.
At least it is when we're the ones who run it.

—FEBRUARY 27, 2006

IF GEORGE W. BUSH HAD WORKED UP THE NERVE TO ASK DICK CHENEY TO BE MORE FORTHCOMING ABOUT HIS HUNTING ACCIDENT

"Perhaps there's some more info you could share."
"Not your affair."

"I'm very glad we had this little talk."
"Just take a walk."

—MARCH 13, 2006

ON THE UPROAR OVER ALLOWING A DUBAI GOVERNMENT COMPANY TO RUN AMERICAN PORTS

Of course the terrorism card's been played
By Bush for years now—making us afraid
With orange alerts and constant talk of war.
With that he's scared off criticism for
Those weapons warnings that were proven phonies,
The no-bid deals he handed to his cronies.
The evil ones, he says, are so abhorrent
He has the right to snoop without a warrant.
The threat is grave, he says, so for a while
He's canceled suspects' right to have a trial.
To criticize his reign, he says, appeases
The bad guys, so he does just what he pleases.
To play the scary card has been his tack.
Is he surprised that someone's played it back?

—MARCH 20, 2006

ON THE REPORT BY HOUSE REPUBLICANS (YES, REPUBLICANS) THAT EXCORIATES THE BUSH ADMINISTRATION FOR ITS FUMBLING RESPONSE TO HURRICANE KATRINA

Though Bushmen had claimed that word never reached
The White House that levees had finally been breached,
The White House was told, all the evidence shows.
Yes, this report shows that it's doubtless that those
In charge of tornadoes and floods and nor'easters
Had all been informed and then sat on their keisters.
And Chertoff was sluggish and clueless and worse.
It's in the report, all in chapter and verse:
His failure to get what the crisis demanded,
Like buses and boats, meant that thousands were stranded.
While Bush, at the ranch, kept on cutting out brush,
His gaggle of clowns seemed to be in no rush.
So Brownie is hardly unique in this mob.
No, others as well did a heckuva job.
It's easy to blame one incompetent slob,
But others as well did a heckuva job.

—MARCH 6, 2006

part 11

The War in
Three Steps

I DREAMT THAT GEORGE W. BUSH ADOPTED JAMES FREY'S THREE-STEP PROGRAM—DENIAL, LARRY KING, AND OPRAH—TO GET TO THE TRUTH ABOUT THE WAR IN IRAQ

STEP ONE:

At first, when people said he'd lied,
He, bristling visibly, denied
A lie or even a mistake
In anything he did to take
This country into a debacle
That, like a nasty streptococcal
Disease, seems endless and resists
The many cures that he insists
Will someday get us unensnared,
While in his speeches he declared
That people saying he misled
Just help the folks who want us dead.

STEP TWO:

This Larry King's a friendly sort,
Who won't object if guests distort
The truth a bit, so pols all like
To make announcements at his mike.
Though presidents don't usually come,
I see Bush there, admitting some
Of what he said was slightly wrong.
Like Frey, he's brought his mom along.
She smiles. He's sounding slightly whiny

While claiming falsehoods all were tiny—
Just unimportant details. And he
Says otherwise the war's just dandy.

STEP THREE:
Our Oprah, stern-faced, draws applause
With questions while he hems and haws.
She clears the mist that still enshrouds
His yellowcake and mushroom clouds.
She asks why, in the name of heaven,
He tied Iraq to 9/11.
Bush stares at her—a hollow stare.
He's all alone. His mom's not there.
He then admits, with eyes quite full,
His tales have been all cock-and-bull.
And Oprah says, "Well, fine. That's great.
For thousands, though, it comes too late."

—FEBRUARY 20, 2006

ABOUT THE AUTHOR

CALVIN TRILLIN, who became *The Nation*'s "deadline poet" in 1990, has also written verse on the events of the day for *The New Yorker, The New York Times,* and National Public Radio. He says he believes in an inclusive political system that prohibits from public office only those whose names have awkward meter or are difficult to rhyme.

ABOUT THE TYPE

The text of this book is set in a sans serif face called Meta. One of the new modern faces of the past twenty years, it was designed by Erik Spiekermann. Meta was originally conceived for the German subway system, but quickly has become one of the most popular typefaces and is often seen in magazines and books.